IN QUIETNESS

In Quietness

An Affirmative Word for More Confident Living

MABEL BURLINGHAM

ZEITGEIST WEST
TUCSON, ARIZONA

Published by
Zeitgeist West

ISBN 978-0-9796921-0-9

Library of Congress Control Number: 2007930942

Burlingham, Mabel Claire Root (1882-1961)

For information or additional copies, contact:

Zeitgeist West
P.O. Box 16472
Tucson, Arizona 85732-6472
zeitgeistwest@gmail.com

Printed in the United States of America
Book Design by Kimura/Bingham Design
Cover Photo: Mabel Burlingham, circa 1948

In quietness and in confidence shall be your strength.

Isaiah 30:15

An affirmative word for more confident living and a scrapbook for your own inspiration.

Mabel Burlingham

CONTENTS

INSPIRATION

O, Life! If I could give you back the Joy
That surges through my heart today,
If I could voice the song that sings within,
The very stones would vibrate with the lay.

If I could give you back the Faith in every man
That leaps within my breast,
If I could breathe my hope for all mankind,
The weary heart of earth would find its rest.

If I could give you back the Loveliness
Which every day unfolds before my sight,
If I could lift the veil on my heart's shrine,
The radiance would dispel the night.

If I could give you back the Love
That fills my soul with Peace Divine,
Then would I wait in silence for Thy Voice,
And lose myself, becoming Thine.

Awareness

So close, and yet beyond my sight,
I sense another world
Of Beauty and of Light.
It seems to permeate the earth
And fill the sky,
It floats upon the clouds
As they pass by.
It ripples on the stream
And murmurs in the breeze,
It sings its sweet refrain
From topmost boughs of trees.
It gleams upon the earth,
And hovers in the air,
It glows within my heart—
God's Love is everywhere!

PEACE

What is this melody that sings within my heart,
With faint reverberation from another sphere?
If I could still the tumult of my thoughts,
I know that heavenly music would come near.

What is this Light that sheds its rays on me,
This Flame that burns within my breast?
The Light that came through sorrow and love's pain,
And lit the flame by which my life is blest.

What is this Love that holds me ever close,
This sweet enchantment promising release?
I yield my little will to Thee, my Lord,
And know, in this submission, there is Peace.

AFFIRMATION

Journeying ever toward perfection,
Though unmindful of his goal,
Man is led by Love's direction,
To the pathway of the soul.

Underneath the sham and pretense,
World confusion, fearful strife,
Is the Voice of Affirmation,
And the harmony of life.

It is here, forever waiting,
Ages old, yet young as spring,
Cosmic song of all creation,
In man's heart begins to sing.

Immortality

There is a purer state of life and being,
A world within the world we know,
A realm where Love and Brotherhood exist,
A refuge for the soul from every foe.

No sense of lack or insecurity,
No fear of what the day may have in store
Can dim the certainty of life unfolding,
Where hate and war and strife exist no more.

All life is moving slowly toward completion,
Man cannot remain in ignorance and sin,
Out of travail and pain, his soul emerging,
He finds the Kingdom of Heaven Is Within.

ADORATION

O Word of Love and Life!
Speak through my eager heart,
With cadence of delight,
Thy secret to impart.

Arouse me when I sleep,
Awake anew my soul's desire,
To seek and find Thee everywhere,
Even to the gate of heaven aspire.

O Word! Rest softly on my heart,
As gentle as a dove,
In silence let it speak
The wonder of Thy love!

Thy Word, my adoration,
Fearless, I take my stand for Thee,
And know, that I, in spite of dire prediction,
Can trust the Soul through all eternity.

The Awakening

In the sacred silence of the heart,
A Voice is calling,
Its low, insistent murmur,
Trembles on the ear,
Faint melody upon the wind
Is singing,
The time of The Awakening,
Is drawing near.

Within the soul of man
New life is stirring,
Awareness of his own true worth
Becoming clear.
Aroused, he breaks the shackles
Of his serfdom, and lo,
He finds, within himself,
The Love that casts out fear.

Resurrection

I stand in the arena of both dire and beautiful experience,
Nor ask for peace nor for the stilling of my pain,
Until the Light Within dispels the darkness,
And sets me firmly on the path again.

I'll take whatever comes with gladness,
Treading the small old path that leads to heaven's domain,
Accepting one by one life's trials and tribulations,
Knowing that all rebellion is in vain.

Through the long vista of days and night unending,
Move shadowy forms with Light and Vision blest,
Forerunners of the God in Man, triumphant,
One shining Figure leading all the rest.

Again the hour of Resurrection
Strikes its clear note of hope on Easter morn,
All nature sings the glad song of creation—
Eternal Spring waits breathless to be born.

INVOCATION

Thou beautiful, sustaining Power,
That holds all life in Thy embrace,
And fills with joy the shining hour
Illumined by Thy Grace.

Thou beautiful, creative Light,
Source of all birth and growth and glad fruition,
Source of our hope and faith, thru darkest night,
To Thy Will, alone, be our submission.

Spirit of Love, Thou Beautiful Necessity,
Blessing all life, building a world more fair,
Restore to human hearts Thy Purity,
That Brotherhood may blossom there.

Realization

If I could peer into the dim Unknown
For one brief moment, see with clearer sight,
I know I would discern loved faces of the past,
Still living, still turning to the Light.

If I could sit in quietness alone,
My mind attuned to silence and repose,
I know the stillness would become articulate,
Revealing what my heart already knows.

If I could hold all life as sacred,
Believing in the dignity and worth of every soul
United in a vast, eternal Brotherhood,
Then I would know, with certainty, The Goal.

LOVE

Thou art the bird in the nest,
The flight, the song.
Thou art the gentle breeze,
The wind so strong.
Thou art the bud, the flower,
The fragrance sweet,
Thou art the sky above,
The earth beneath my feet.

Thou art the gleam of dawn,
The setting sun,
Thou art my heart's deep peace,
When day is done.
Thou art the rippling stream,
The ocean's roar,
Thou art the still small voice
That calls me evermore

And bids me not to seek afar,
Nor to embrace an ancient creed,
But worship at Thy Beauty's shrine,
Finding in Thee my only need.
For Thou art Love, the Inner Light,
Shining in darkness thru the night.
The Love in every heart concealed,
Waiting Thy Touch alone to be revealed.

ETERNAL SPRING

Light on the far horizon gleaming,
Rustle of wings in the vibrant air,
Glad intimations of new life stirring,
Worship, the heart's cry everywhere.

Voice of hope on the wind ascending,
Rhythm of life, the soul's refrain,
Tuned to the love-motif of heaven,
Childlike faith in the heart again.

Clearer sense of a growing purpose,
New life springing joyous and free,
Out of darkness, slowly emerging,
Lover of God and Humanity.

UNFOLDMENT

Man was made for joy, not pleasure,
He was created for happiness beyond his own,
The very fibre of his soul containing
Divine Unfoldment, God's gift to him alone.

Man was created to be a lover,
Giving with no thought of return,
Trusting to Love's unfailing guidance,
Each man's truth that he must learn.

God is Love and all creation springs
From His Pure Thought Sublime,
Birth and growth and procreation,
All reflect His Love Divine.

Slowly, surely, life evolving,
New insights on quickened minds,
Reveal a wondrous plan and purpose,
When man, through Love, his own soul finds.

MY PRAYER

Keep me aglow with thoughts of Thee,
Help me to know serenity,
Whether I rest or work or pray,
Let me be with Thee night and day.

Keep me responsive to Thy Will,
The voice of self within me still,
And, in the Silence, to my soul impart,
The deeper understanding of the heart.

The Song of Life

In every fragrant flower that by the wayside blooms,
In every lark who flings on high his merry tunes,
In every lamb who gambols on the grassy sod,
Let me be conscious of the Love of God.

In sunlight streaming through the trees,
In hum of nectar-laden bees,
In gentle rain that falls from heaven above,
Let me be conscious of His Love.

The sunlit earth by day, the stars by night
Reveal the glory of Eternal Light,
And in the radiant face of childhood, let me see
The Vision of His Immortality.

Salvation

Into that Greater Life, my little life expanding,
Lifted to heights beyond my mortal sight,
Only my heart assures me of a Presence,
Leading me swiftly upward toward the Light.

The Greater Life is all around us,
Seeking to penetrate our very own.
We have to live and love and pray into it,
Until at last we find ourselves at home.

There is no spot on earth, however distant,
There is no life, however steeped in sin
Beyond His Love and His Forgiveness;
However dark, His Light can enter in.

ASSURANCE

To every soul who questions life,
And seeks an answer to the great Unknown,
There comes assurance of an inner guide,
A feeling one is not alone.

And every truth we need to know,
And every prayer, sincere and true
For greater light, is answered,
A book, a poem or a friend, may be the avenue.

A little love, a little faith,
A little quietness amidst the din,
And human hearts, so lonely and afraid,
Are lifted to the Heaven Within.

ETERNAL LIGHT

Lord, keep me loving, praising, worshipping,
I feel Thy Presence near.
No need to voice my longing,
Each mute appeal, You hear.

No need for me to plead for help,
Nor gifts upon Thine altar lay,
Thou who art nearer than my breath,
Know my heart's need before I pray.

My need alone is just for Thee,
To see Thy world with inner sight,
To walk with Thee and do Thy Will,
And follow the Eternal Light.

The truth that Christ revealed to man,
In simple words and selfless deeds,
God's Love and Brotherhood of Man—
The only truth this sad world needs.

TRANSCENDENCE

Wings and the blue empyrean,
The soul in flight,
Gone the illusion of life's delirium,
Banished the night.

Light and the flaming instant,
Heaven revealing,
Ease to the heart unresistant,
Tender the feeling.

Trust in an Infinite Love,
Gentle The Presence,
Creative Power from above,
Emerged, The Transcendence.

Eternal Moment

Only Eternity is long enough
To reach the heights of Being,
Where God His Watch is keeping,
And Heaven awaits the soul.

In Silence, self-transcending,
The heart is tuned to gladness,
No room is there for sadness,
In the Everlasting Joy.

Only Eternity can hold
Such Love as Being knows,
Our lives and everything that grows,
His Tenderness enfolds.

So great a Purpose
Must He have in mind,
Such Blessedness for all mankind,
Awaits the Hour of Revelation.

Each moment holds Eternity:
All life is One.
To every heart, Thy Kingdom Come,
That we may know Reality.

EXALTATION

I have fallen in love with Thy Beauty, my darling,
I saw it revealed in a garden fair,
The tiniest jewels of the whole plant kingdom,
Nestled in radiant loveliness there.

I have fallen in love with Thy Goodness, my darling,
I see it reflected in human life,
The deep, sweet flow of its healing waters
Will cleanse man's soul, and end all strife.

I have fallen in love with Life, my darling,
I see Thee inherent in the veriest clod.
Beauty, itself, is the end of living,
And Beauty, itself, is the Face of God.

Mabel Claire Root Burlingham
(1882-1961)

> *We do well whatever we love to do, and all good work*
> *is beautiful and ennobling, no matter how humble it is.*
>
> *Mabel Burlingham*

Mabel Burlingham was a poet, intellectual, inventor, gardener and artist. Like many American women of her generation coming of age at the turn of the century, she struggled with finding the path to her true, most expressive self. In spite of social and political conditions that limited the role of women, she never lost faith in the creative life process and the possibilities that are latent in every human heart.

Born in Bloomington, Illinois in 1882, Mabel Burlingham moved to Syracuse in 1900 to live with her sister Grace Root Bausch, her husband George and their two young children. In 1908, she married Dr. James P. Burlingham, a practicing osteopathic physician. The young couple made their home in Syracuse where Dr. Burlingham later developed an internationally celebrated garden of rare alpine plants.

The couple raised three children: Robert, a poet like his mother and later a journalist at Fortune Magazine; Margaret, a professional home economist, creator of "The Homemaker's Scrapbook" and owner of her own home-based food business; and James, a chemical engineer for DuPont, an avid collector of alpine and native plants, and an active member of the American Rock Garden Society.

Mabel Burlingham had wide-ranging intellectual interests with a particular passion for religion, mysticism, and poetry. Her religious faith and positive philosophy of living was articulated in guest columns in the Syracuse Post-Standard and in her prolific essays and poetry. Mabel Burlingham's friends were intellectual leaders of the time including educator Madame Maria Montessori, Bahá'í thinkers Howard and Mable Ives, author Dhan Gopal Mukerji, and editor and peace activist Norman Cousins. Mabel Burlingham traveled across the United States with Maria Montessori, and started the first Montessori school in Syracuse when she returned.

After Dr. Burlingham's death in 1939, jelly and jewelry gave Mabel a career. She founded the Cinnama-Tang Products Company and invented a formula for cinnamon syrup and jellies, sold all over the U.S. She also created distinctive beaded earrings that retailed in the finest shops in New York, Chicago, and California.

In 1949, the Syracuse Post-Standard cited Mabel Burlingham as one of the city's "10 Women of Achievement." Articles and columns about her appeared in *The New York Herald Tribune, The New York Times, The Christian Science Monitor,* the *Ladies Home Journal,* and other newspapers and magazines.

In a 1954 article Mabel Burlingham noted that "The need to express oneself creatively is the most urgent need in human life." The topic of that essay was hobby shops, crafts and cooking, but her philosophical focus was the *art spirit*:

> *The art spirit is something that affects the lives of every one of us. You do not need to be a painter or a sculptor to do any outstanding work of genius to be an artist in the true sense of the word... The art spirit is at work in the home... Maybe your husband will eat that delectable pie you made with so much care today, without a word of comment, not even a grunt of satisfaction. Never mind, just remember that you touched the realm of pure poetry when you made that pie, and the magic of the art spirit is upon you. That is enough to illumine your day...*

The least little task becomes an exciting adventure, for life begins to take on new meaning when it is realized that the creative spirit is essentially love in action. We do well whatever we love to do, and all good work is beautiful and ennobling, no matter how humble it is.

Mabel Burlingham spent the last years of her life in Cohasset, Massachusetts with her daughter Margaret Scheuren and family. Until her death in 1961, she lived her life in tune with the creative spirit.

In Quietness expresses Mabel Burlingham's abiding religious faith and hope that her poems would always serve as an "affirmative word for more confident living."

MABEL BURLINGHAM

FAMILY PHOTOGRAPHS, ARTICLES AND LETTERS

Mabel Burlingham in her Syracuse home, circa 1918

Mabel Burlingham with her children Margaret and Robert, circa 1914

L to R: Margaret, James, Jr. and Mabel Burlingham, circa 1941

L to R: Robert, Mabel, and Margaret Burlingham, circa 1938

Burlingham Garden under construction in 1920

Lily pond in Burlingham Garden, circa 1930

Mabel Burlingham in the garden, circa 1935

Dr. James P. Burlingham in the garden, circa 1935

Dwarf Alpine Crocus Bed Is in Bloom In Burlingham Memorial Garden

FIRST SPRING CROCUS at Burlingham Memorial Garden is examined by Mrs. James P. Burlingham. Rare plants from all parts of the world stock the famed beauty spot.

April 3, 1941 Syracuse Herald Journal. Reproduced with permission of The Post-Standard.

Mrs. Mabel C. Burlingham and the double trillium for which a mouse acted as stork.

August 10, 1941 The Post-Standard. Reproduced with permission.

Window of Merchant's National Bank in Syracuse, New York, 1952

Both Jelly and Jewelry Give Kindly Housewife a Career

By Jessie Ash Arndt (Woman's Editor of The Christian Science Monitor)

Jelly and jewelry have little relation in the minds of most people but for Mrs. Mabel C. Burlingham of Syracuse, N.Y., those two words are synonyms for business success.

First came the jelly. Mrs. Burlingham had made it ever since she went to housekeeping years ago; but in 1941, she experimented with cinnamon flavor in apple jelly. It gave an unusual tang to it, and the color was a ruby red.

She also made an unusually fine mint jelly with a delicious tang to it and a color as clear as an emerald. Like many neighborly and generous homemakers, she always had little jars on hand to give to friends at Christmas or on other special occasions.

"Mabel, you should go into business, this is the best jelly I've ever tasted," her friends told her time and again. "Well mother, why don't you?" insisted her daughter who was then Director of Home Service in Syracuse for the Central New York Light and Power Company.

Daughter Helped at First

"Daughter was my spark plug in the beginning," Mrs. Burlingham told me as she displayed the sparkling jars of red and green jelly. So she starting selling in and around Syracuse. The labels read Cinnama-tang and Mint-tang Jelly, and her first order was from a Syracuse store to which her daughter took samples.

But the rapid growth in her business outside that area, came in a roundabout way, actually through a story she wrote for a horticultural magazine about an unusual flower in her garden.

This little article brought an out-of-town visitor to see the flower. But what interested him equally was the jelly which he saw on her dining table. "Why my wife and I started just this way making applesauce years ago," he told her, recounting the success which had followed their early venture in the food business.

Through his interest and advice, Mrs. Burlingham made contacts with stores in other cities which handled such delicacies. Among them was the old and famous S.S. Pierce Store of Boston which one Christmas ordered more than her sugar supply would provide.

Likes Own Kitchen Best

She expanded her equipment somewhat, obtaining a GI kettle with a faucet, with the aid of which she can make 10 dozen small jars of jelly at a time. But she still uses her own rather small kitchen with its gas range, table, and sink all within easy reach, and says she doesn't want to have larger quarters.

Most of the work she does herself, but when orders crowd in, she asks two good friends to come over and help her. They do this eagerly, wiping and labeling the jars for her, and putting them in the boxes piled up on the dining table. In this way she can make 40 dozen jars a day.

She serves lunch for her friends and repays them with a gift of something she knows they want or will enjoy, but their assistance is all on a friendly rather than a business basis. They consider it good fun to work with her and it always makes the day, as well as the work, go faster for her to have them over.

Both Busy and Generous

It was during the last year of the war that short sugar rations curtailed Mrs. Burlingham's jelly-making and resulting in long intervals when she could not put out her product. Again, just to be busy and have little gifts for her friends, she began making bead earrings. Discovering a box of beads which she had saved over the years, simply because she liked beads and never wanted to throw any away, she experimented with them, inspired by a bead choker a friend of hers had made.

The results of her experiments surprised her. She thought they were good enough to improve and market. With confidence born of her successful jelly project, she went to New York, bought beads better adapted to jewelry-making than those she had and went to work designing earrings.

After making 50 to 75 designs, she let her daughter take them for her to an exclusive shop in Syracuse. She received a prompt order. Then she ventured into New York City with them. To her delight she sold a large order to Lord & Taylor. Later, Filene's in Boston also put them in stock, and nothing gives this jewelry-jelly designer more of a thrill than to see her delicately designed earrings and sparkling jellies in the display cases of the leading stores that handle them.

Every Design is New

The earrings are in an unlimited number of designs and beautiful color combinations. "I never think of copying, for every time I begin to work and experiment, a new design comes to me. They are as different as snowflakes by their delicacy and their sparkle.

They are perfectly made and somewhere in each one is a bead or combination of beads to catch the light and give life to the design. And of course they are by no means an inexpensive item at a costume-jewelry counter.

So successful has Mrs. Burlingham been in her two widely different ventures that she has been called upon to relate her success story in Buffalo, Rochester, and elsewhere in New York State at the Career Clinics of the Women's Council of the New York State Department of Commerce.

She believes that every woman has some special talent which should find an outlet in just such marketable endeavor as she has carried on for the past seven years. Her children are grown with homes of their own and she has her own career – perhaps the kind she might have thought of somewhat wistfully years earlier when she was giving all her time and thought to her home and family.

Housewife's Pancake Syrup Experiment
Results in Cinama-tang, New Flavoring

Cinama-tang. Cinama-tang.

Say it over to yourself a few times. Get familiar with the word. Chances are you'll soon be saying it as frequently as you say chocolate, vanilla or strawberry.

Mrs. James P. Burlingham of 206 Rugby Rd. hopes you'll be saying it more frequently, because she is the inventor of cinama-tang. It is a new flavor, one that she accidentally discovered in her own kitchen and one that has recently been put on the market commercially.

Cinama-tang – its formula is secret, of course – is described by Mrs. Burlingham as "a blend, with cinnamon predominating."

"It has a spicy and a refreshing taste," she continues, "but the one word that describes it best is 'tangy'."

SPREADS OUT OF CITY

Ice cream companies in Syracuse first became interested in it, but its popularity is fast spreading. It is also being sold now in Washington, D.C.; Philadelphia, Pa., and other large cities. A leading ice cream company with many outlets in New York city has just contracted to buy large amounts of the flavoring, and soon the metropolitan gourmets will be eating their cinama-tang ice cream cones and sodas.

Mrs. Burlingham also expects her new flavor to be introduced on a large scale in the New England states.

The story of the discovery of cinama-tang is an interesting one.

"I've always been a homebody," explains Mrs. Burlingham. "But I've always been interested in experimenting with my cooking and in getting new flavors and new recipes."

HOW IT HAPPENED

"One day, around Christmas, I think it was, I was trying to get something besides the ordinary maple taste in my pancakes and waffles. I wanted something sort of spicy. And from that experimentation, I got this syrup."

Mrs. Burlingham began using the syrup, in different densities, in ice creams, desserts, puddings, jellies, and in cooking and baking generally.

One day a friend, visiting her from New York city, suggested that the flavor had good commercial possibilities. Mrs. Burlingham accepted the suggestion.

She enlisted the aid of her son, James, who is studying chemical engineering at Cornell university. His knowledge of chemistry helped in the promotion and commercialization of the product.

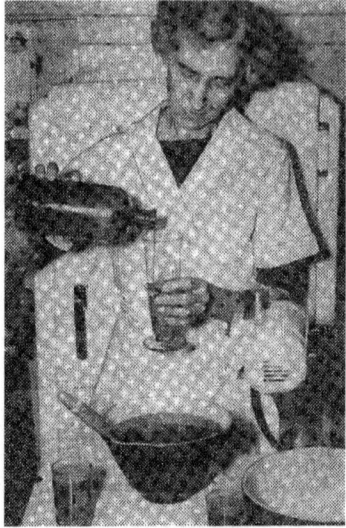

A dash of this and a dash of that and stir it just so much – and Mrs. James P. Burlingham of 206 Rugby Rd. has a sample of the new ice cream flavor she invented, cinama-tang.

OTHERS LIKE TASTE

"Word of the flavor spread," Mrs. Burlingham continues. "Soon one of the Syracuse ice cream companies approached me, and asked to try it. They said they had astonishingly good results, and wanted more of the syrup. After a while, other companies approached me, and I approached others."

The syrup – its name copyrighted and its formula secret – is now being made by a Syracuse company. Cinama-tang has outgrown the confines of Mrs. Burlingham's kitchen.

The flavoring produces a pink color – quite distinctive from strawberry – in ice cream. But Mrs. Burlingham is enthusiastic about its many possibilities besides as an ice cream flavoring. The makers of candies, pastries, jellies and a number of desserts are interested, and while the financial returns are still in the "none-too-great" stage, the odds are that Mrs. Burlingham will be well repaid for her waffles-and-pancakes experiment of last Christmas.

June 9, 1940 The Post-Standard. Reproduced with permission.

THE WHITE HOUSE
WASHINGTON

July 19, 1940

My dear Mrs. Burlingham:

        The ice-cream which you had sent
to me from Washington arrived in good con-
dition and was very much enjoyed.

        Thank you very much for your
kindness.

                Sincerely yours,

                Eleanor Roosevelt

June 19, 1940 Letter to Mabel Burlingham from Eleanor Roosevelt

Mrs. Burlingham in TV Debut
Describes Her Jam, Jewelry

Syracuse's eternally youthful grandmother, Mrs. Mabel Burlingham, who has developed not one but two small business careers after 60, made her television debut Tuesday in New York City on the Margaret Arlen program.

Describing her jam and jewelry business which has been developed over the past several years, Mrs. Burlingham demonstrated to the Arlen listeners that small business can be good sense for women who want to earn extra money.

Mrs. Burlingham was chosen to appear on the program, a new series demonstrating the achievements of women in developing businesses of their own, from a list of success stories compiled and developed by the Woman's Program, The New York State Department of Commerce.

Mrs. Burlingam was a "success story" speaker at the Woman's program "Business of Her Own" clinic in Syracuse in 1949. She will exhibit her jams and her jewelry June 14 at a "Business of Her Own" clinic in Watertown, and "Business of Her Own" clinic scheduled for June 21 at Newark.

APPEARS ON TV — Mrs. Mabel Burlingham described her jam and jewelry business on the Margaret Arlen program Tuesday in New York City.

June 8, 1951 The Post-Standard. Reproduced with permission.

FOUNDED 1628

MARBLE COLLEGIATE CHURCH
FIFTH AVENUE AT 29TH STREET, WEST
NEW YORK 1, N. Y.

MINISTERS
NORMAN VINCENT PEALE
HERMAN L. BARBERY
EUGENE MCKINLEY PIERCE

December 18, 1952

Mrs. Mabel C. Burlingham
114 East Colvin St.
Syracuse, New York

Dear Mrs. Burlingham:

Thank you so much for your beautiful and inspiring
poems. I am enjoying the book very much.

Hoping you will worship with us soon again and with
a prayer that God will continue to bless you, I am

Cordially yours,

Norman V. Peale.

NVP:AVM

December 18, 1952 Letter to Mabel Burlingham from Norman Vincent Peale

www.ingramcontent.com/pod-product-compliance
Lightning Source LLC
Chambersburg PA
CBHW031335040426
42443CB00005B/356